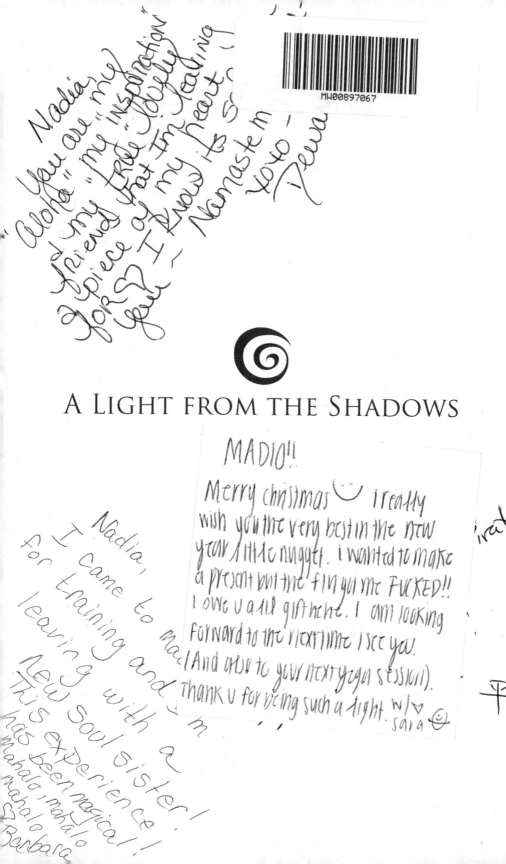

Nadia,
"Aloha" my inspiration ~
my "free flowing"
friend that I'm leading
a piece of my heart
for ~ I know I'm leading
you ~ Namaste in
xoxo ~
Dewa

MW00897067

A LIGHT FROM THE SHADOWS

MADIO!!
Merry christmas ☺ i really
wish you the very best in the new
year little nugget. i wanted to make
a present but the f in you me FUCKED!!
i owe u a lil gift here. I am looking
forward to the next time i see you.
(And also to your next yoga session).
thank u for being such a light. w/♡
- sara 🪐

Nadia,
I came to mai
for training and I'm
leaving with a
NEW soul sister!
This experience
has been magical!
mahalo, mahalo
mahalo
Barbara

A Light from the Shadows:

Reflections on Oneness, Identity, and the Creation of Experience

An Emergence Book
By Eric Micha'el Leventhal

Cover image:
"Rose Galaxy" taken by the Hubble Space Telescope.

Emergence: Holistic Education Services
P.O. Box 81778
Haiku, HI 96708
info@theartofemergence.com

Printed in the United States of America

First Printing, 2012

ISBN-13: 978-1470103767

ISBN-10: 1470103761

To Asherah,
who found me in the Dream
and stayed for the waking.

"All that is gold does not glitter,
Not all those who wander are lost;
The old that is strong does not wither,
Deep roots are not reached by the frost.

From the ashes a fire shall be woken,
A light from the shadows shall spring;
Renewed shall be blade that was broken,
The crownless again shall be king."

— J.R.R. Tolkien, *The Fellowship of the Ring*

"Thought with totality as its content has to be considered as an art form, like poetry, whose function is primarily to give rise to a new perception, rather than to communicate reflective knowledge of 'how everything is.'

This implies that there can no more be an ultimate form of such thought than there could be an ultimate poem (that would make all further poems unnecessary)."

— David Bohm, *Wholeness and the Implicate Order*

Contents

Preface

This collection of 108 original poems, essays and aphorisms emerged over a period of nine months through the dedicated medium of online social networking.

The author wishes to convey profound gratitude to all those who continue to contribute their time, attention, and open-hearted curiosity to the collectively sustained unfoldment of the ideas contained in these pages.

For more information, please visit
www.alightfromtheshadows.com

Preamble:
A Declaration of Independent Thought

We hold these truths to be self-evident, that all beings are created equal, that we are endowed by and as our creators with certain unalienable rights, that among these are love, consciousness and the pursuit of authenticity.

That to secure these rights, belief systems are instituted among human beings, deriving their just powers from the consent of the faithful. That whenever any form of thought becomes destructive to these ends, it is our right to alter or to abolish it, and to institute new perception, laying its foundation on such principles and organizing its powers in such form, as to us shall seem most likely to effect our freedom and enlightenment.

Prudence, indeed, will dictate that beliefs long established should not be changed for light and transient causes; and accordingly all experience hath shown that humankind are more disposed to suffer, while evils are sufferable, than to right ourselves by abolishing the thought-forms to which we are accustomed.

But when a long train of abuses and usurpations, pursuing invariably the same object evinces a design to reduce us under absolute despotism, it is our right, it is our duty, to throw off such convictions, and to provide new guards for our future well-being.

CREATION

Though the process may itself be steeped in shadow,
understand that at this very moment,
in some clear and vital chamber of your being,
you are choosing to experience those aspects of yourself
whose perfection you have still to discover.

The nature of this game
is one of responding to the world around you
until you come to realize
that the world is responding to you.

At each moment,
our seemingly objective world emerges
from the dancing of consciousness
with a single untruth:

that there is something out there
which is not us.

The sacred stillness of your brilliant heart
has as the myriad wonders masqueraded.
But if you knew this secret from the start,
then you'd have quit this Game before you played it.

As you begin to look deeply
into the mystery of your own evolution,
in place of good and evil you will find only stories,
finished or unfinished.

The stories you believe to be true
are the ones your life will become.

We do not see things as they are,
nor do we even see them as we are,
but only as we believe our story to have been.

All stories are born out of illusion,
but that doesn't mean they're not worth telling.

The infinite play of human reality
emerges from a single illusion:
that somehow the one who reads these words
is not the one who writes them.

The shortest interval between two points
is the awareness that they are not two.

From a universal perspective,
what you do matters less
than how you feel
about what you do.

Our task and challenge as human beings
is to appreciate, in the same instant,
both the infinite significance
and absolute insignificance of life.

A Lesson from the Void:

Just because you're not aware,
doesn't mean it isn't there.
Just because your mind can't take it,
doesn't mean Life didn't make it.

On this, my friends, we can agree:
that what you get is what you see.
The thoughts behind the life you dream
may be more real than who you seem.

Each day, we dream into being the parts of ourselves
that we are still learning to love.

And each day,
without effort or knowing,
we ourselves become the space
through which our stories emerge into causality,
until we no longer choose to create ourselves within them.

RE·AL·IZE [ree-uh-lahyz]

1. to grasp or understand clearly.
2. to make real; give reality to.

Any questions?

FLOW

Synchronicity is the soul's reminder of authorship.

We view and interpret the events of our lives
according to the beliefs we hold about ourselves.

Our perceiving minds operate under the illusion of a time-based causality — the belief that the past gives rise to the present, and the present to an inexorable future.

In reality, it is the *idea* of our presence in the universal mind that ultimately initiates and underlies the circumstances of our existence.

Everything in existence begins as an idea, and every idea naturally seeks expression in as many dimensions as possible, from the imaginal to the actual.

When an idea takes hold in the universal mind, its presence automatically gives rise to a series of circumstances and events which facilitate its unfoldment in material reality.

So if you want to experience a new reality,
then it's time to change your mind.

A peaceful mind appreciates the present moment
as the living embodiment of naked perfection,
rather than a means to future attainment.

And when you see all places as the same,
then time itself begins to disappear.

For it takes time to go from here to there,
and yet no time at all from here to here.

Although we may believe
that our future is determined by what we do now,
the future is actually born from our attachment
to past experience.

When we forgive the events of our past,
we also release the subtle necessity
of creating future opportunities
for their re-enactment.

And all that remains for us then
is an eternal present.

Time itself is only as real
as your own mental discrimination
between the revelation and concealment
of the one Light.

Without emotion,
all is motionless.

The events that our minds perceive
as linear cause and effect
can be imagined as points
along a spiral of becoming.

True cause is not to be found
along this spiral of perceived events,
but within the idea or being
whose emergence the spiral intends to manifest.

What characteristics does humanity typically ascribe to divinity?

Omnipotence. Omniscience. Omnipresence.
"Omni-" as in "all," as in the complete absence of limitation.

Yet in projecting our concept of this infinite presence and power outward, we inadvertently come to define ourselves in terms of our perceived distance from this same ideal.

In story, when a god wishes something into being, that thing is bound to arise instantaneously. And yet our experience tells us that something has to happen — that certain events have to *transpire* — before our own desires can be fulfilled.

But why should it be so?

If we are truly gods, as the great esoteric traditions of the world affirm us to be, then why should we need to labor towards an unforeseen future before resting in the perfection of our own desire?

The reality is that upon conception our desires begin automatically to materialize, and yet in order for the mind to accept the fact of their manifestation, it dutifully sets its creative energies to informing and animating the ensuing story of how what we wanted came to be.

Having borne witness to the material fulfillment of our desire, the mind proceeds to construe and review an associated series of storylike events, so that we say, "Ah yes, that's the reason I went to that place, why I met that person there, why I had to endure that suffering, etc. It all happened for a reason...."

In truth, however, that reason is not to be found in the events of any perceived story, but in the <u>desire</u> that gives rise to them. In the meantime, the spiral of your unfolding narrative provides a familiar semblance of causality, which in turn allows your mind to accept the change as having really occurred.

When you see that your desire alone "causes" the change, you begin to relax your dependence on the mental narrative to explain or justify the appearance of that change. And as you enter into an awareness of your own divinity, you begin also to surrender your need for time to divide conception from creation, thought from experience.

And then the question becomes:

How much time do you wish to endure,
before you allow the change to occur?

Sometimes it takes a miracle to remind us
that the only permanent condition
is that of impermanence.

STRUGGLE

Transform your desire into love,
and limits start to lose their usefulness.

Our experience of suffering is the greatest obstacle
on the path to remembering our identity
with and as infinite creation.

Dividing our life experiences into positive and negative,
we tend to reason:

"If I really were the creator of my own life,
why would I create negative experiences for myself?
I wouldn't, therefore something outside of me
must be creating the world I experience."

But rather than dismiss the question of your own infinite
nature, you've got to go further and ask:

"If I truly were a being of infinite creativity and love,
why would I create suffering and limitation
for myself?"

And only you can answer that question.

Whether or not you are aware of it,
your sense of a separate, unique, and familiar identity
would dissolve without the binding force
of your suffering.

If you wish to return
to an awareness of your limitless identity,
then begin to see the ways you choose to suffer,
and simply choose not to.

Every story contains an element of struggle.
Who would you be without yours?

When we judge or resist an aspect of our life experience,
we tend to formulate a proportionate sense of identity
in polarity with that same aspect of consciousness.

If this seemingly negative aspect of consciousness
were to vanish from our experience,
then our familiar sense of identity
would vanish along with it.

For this reason,
the aspects of ourselves
that we deny the most passionately
are also the hardest ones to relinquish.

Resistance is the subtlest form of attachment.

What people say about you
doesn't say anything about you,
but it does say something about them.

To experience a new reality
you must know,
not only that change is possible,
but that you deserve it.

All fear is rooted in the belief
that love could somehow be limited,
yet no such limitation actually exists
outside of our own minds.

The only thing we need to heal
is the belief that we are not already whole.

Suffering occurs
when love's two hands pull your soul
in two directions.

The way to end disease
is by realizing that it never existed to begin with.

Understand that right now, in this moment,
you both have and are everything
that the recognized and unrecognized aspects of yourself
simultaneously desire to experience.

If the objects of your desire appear to elude you,
then begin to notice and acknowledge your subtle desire
to experience their opposites.

Miracles can only inhabit the reality of our awareness
when we surrender our need for the familiar
to our desire for the limitless.

Until you know your identity
with and as the reality of love,
suffering and limitation will remain
as necessary to your existence
as air and water.

If you wish to transform
the conditions of your world,
then begin to notice how you have made suffering
into a condition of your own existence.

The next time something unpleasant
appears to occur outside of you,
ask how you yourself are contributing in this moment,
by your thought, word and action,
to the creation of a world in which suffering must occur
in order for you to recognize yourself.

The purpose of suffering
is to contain the light of your desire
until you see yourself in everything.

Telling yourself to wake up from the Dream
is like telling a drowning person to stop treading water.

When you begin to recognize your own need for limitation,
you will realize that you are also the water,
and that you are already waking.

The blessing of resistance lies in its power
to illuminate those aspects of ourselves
which have eluded our appreciation.

Appreciation is the recognition
that limitation is no longer a condition
of our evolution.

Your struggle lets you know that you exist,
while loving lets you feel your boundlessness.

As an emerging human,
the time has come for you to know,
with your whole being,
that you both exist infinitely
and are loved infinitely.

LOVE

A Prayer for the Digital Age:

May our love of information and of ease
never exceed our love for one another.

AMO ERGO SUM.
(I love, therefore I am.)

Wisdom may teach you that all places are one,
but love shows you how to get there.

I searched for my Beloved
in the strangest of places,
until the day I realized
I couldn't take my eyes off Her.

A human being trying to attract more love
is like a fish trying to attract more water.

The degree of freedom we enjoy outwardly
is a reflection of the degree of love
we cultivate inwardly.

If you want to know
what real love looks like,
first imagine a master and a servant,
then imagine being unable to distinguish between them.

And while the masculine initiates,
the feminine allows and makes the space:
The active and the passive forms of love
emerge below, just as they do above.

Love is
the perception of perfection
beyond the protection of our projection.

Love is the highest form of meditation.

There is no greater treasure in this world
than somebody who loves you as you are.

Love does not mean elevating
another person above yourself,
so much as withdrawing your belief
in the imaginary boundary between you.

If you would choose to place your beloved on a pedestal,
then love would ask you to STEP UP
and be with him or her, until the two of you
no longer recognize any difference
between the pedestal and the ground.

The moment you open yourself completely
to the love that awaits your conscious embrace,
you are no longer there to receive it.

To the ego, love is a poison.

Love is calling you to awaken.

If you would still choose to sleep,
dream of love.

I am the poet who writes from the ashes
of an all-consuming encounter
at the edge of the world.

In those moments
when I myself am filled up with darkness,
with no space even for my own light,
let alone the light of another,
I feel as though the narrow recesses of my being
can scarcely contain your effulgence.

In those moments
I begin to understand the ancient admonition
that warns seekers away from any attempt
to behold God directly,
as though were I to look into the sun of your radiant heart,
the very lens of my perception would shatter,
and there would be nothing left of me.

Your love is the fire and I the wood.

And yet each day with you I remember,
a little more clearly,
that I too am this fire;
that I do not stand in opposition
but am one with that which consumes me.

And so I celebrate my annihilation
and plant seeds of knowing
in the smoldering ruins
of my former mansion.

This is the story of love's encounter with love
at the edge of the world,
and we are the poem that rises from the ashes.

In the end, love is the only story worth believing.

IDENTITY

You are here on earth
to unearth who on earth you are.

The awareness that seeks to know
is the very object of its own seeking.

Our instrumental part in the symphony of life
is to allow love to create a space within our own awareness,
through which the undreamed mystery may emerge
as a knowable reality.

I say:
I am a man. I am happy. I am writing these words...
when really I am none of these things.

It would be more accurate to say
that through my presence, I embody or allow
the expression of each of these states of consciousness.

At this moment, for instance, my presence gives expression
to the male form, to the feeling of happiness,
to the action of writing, etc.

Your essence is equally beyond definition,
beyond the polarities of male and female,
beyond the rhythmic sway
of human emotion and experience.

The moment you say that you ARE one of these states,
you begin to define yourself according to its qualities.

And once you do so,
it can become very, very difficult
to discern your real self from the particular qualities
of that familiar expression of consciousness.

To embody the miracle of the new,
there is no need to change who you are.

The only question to ask is:

Which energies have you allowed to emerge
through the vessel of your presence up until this moment,
and which ones do you now desire to experience?

The fearful seek to serve themselves by mastering the world,
while the fearless seek to serve the world
by mastering themselves.

Craving sustenance,
the sage knows: I am this food.
Are you still hungry?

Intention unfolds at the point of meeting
between the desire for experience
and the awareness of identity.

To know the world,
you must reveal yourself.

The evolution of the universe
is both mirrored by and incumbent upon your own.

With or without our knowledge,
we are all alchemists.

Your life is an idea in the universal mind . . .

Make it a good one.

A thought cannot be understood
by a mind unwilling to contain it.

You are that uncontainable thought.

So if you would know yourself,
then you must be willing to empty your mind
of everything you thought yourself to be.

To free yourself from the known,
you yourself must know:

Your story doesn't make you who you are —
it's who you are that makes your story what it is.

Sooner or later on this journey,
every traveler faces the same question:

Are you a human intending to be a god,
or a god pretending to be human?

In our need to be somebody,
we often forget that we are somebody.

No matter how strange things get,
know that with every breath you are becoming
that which you have always been.

Perhaps the greatest irony of human life
is the belief that we already know ourselves,
when who we are is waiting in the wings.

You are blessed
to have been ignorant of your own beauty
until now.

For if you had known of it,
if you had already allowed yourself
to feel and open to this light,

captivated and contented,

you would have lost all interest in the things of this world,
and our shared existence would be immensely darkened
by the shadow of your absence.

Search not for happiness outside yourself,
for nothing could be further from the truth.

I am not an indigo child.
I am not a rainbow warrior.
I am not a galactic starseed.
I am not an ascended master.

I am the ocean of infinite consciousness,
or I am nothing at all.

The path to God begins and ends with you.

VISION

If you want to see,
then begin to see
how you see.

The way to embody love completely
is to see and appreciate life just as it is,
and not as you believe, fear, or desire it to be.

Waking up begins by understanding
that you are not in your right mind.

Both your mind and personality are vehicles for the unique
expression of certain universal energies. Through the ever-
emerging play of your life, your mind and personality lend
themselves to the expression of human polarity: maleness
and femaleness, love and fear, desire and contentment, and
all the other infinite facets of this jewel called Being.

But that does not mean that you <u>are</u> these things, nor that
you need look to them for your identity.

Intrinsic to the expression of these universal energies is a
sense of limitation, for without limitation there would be
no experiencing, no relating. You would not know sound
from silence, day from night, up from down. If you were to
remain eternally in the consciousness that knows it is
everything, then you would be unable to touch the
existence and beauty of the world around you.

The gift of limitation and resistance, then, is to allow you to recognize, to approach and, ultimately, to embody the energies which you have yet to acknowledge as belonging to your own unique expression of Being.

In other words, reality is so completely in love with you that it will restrict its own infinite potential in order to help you discover your own.

The problem comes when you take limitation and suffering to be an intrinsic part of your being, and begin to rely on them in order to recognize yourself.

The way out is to know that limitation is intrinsic to your personality, but not to who you are.

For who you are is beyond description.

To wake up from the dream of limitation,
find the thought in your mind that says,
"I am a limited being,"
and then ask yourself:

Who is thinking that thought?

When you can no longer tell the difference
between being yourself and being love,
you are not far from waking up.

Spirit is in love with Her creations,
and we are here to learn to love Her back.

We can only forgive the world
to the extent that we forgive ourselves for being in it.

The secret to happiness
is to be grateful for every moment of life.

Gratitude is the ultimate form of prayer.

It doesn't matter how you conceive of divinity.
It only matters that you see it in everything,
including yourself.

The purpose of life is to reach a point
where you can say "yes" to all of it.

Acceptance is the vessel of realization.

What you hate, you re-create;
and what you bless, you put to rest.

To experience what isn't,
love what is.

We are at our most powerful
the moment we no longer need to be powerful.

Mastery is the art of merging desire with actuality.

To wake from a dream, you must know that it's over.

ONENESS

To see through the illusion of duality,
remember that fear and darkness
have no substance in themselves,
for they do not indicate the presence
of a second universal force,
but are only names given
to the one Light unperceived.

Our minds see two where there is one;
one life springs up, another done.
Why bless your in and curse your out?
So what is all the fuss about?

New life begins when death sets in . . .

Contracting one, expands another:
Creation and destruction are the most inseparable of lovers.

The more we begin to recognize
the positive in the negative,
the more clearly we come to realize
both their identity and our own.

The breath you spend to curse an enemy
is also spent in blessing your beloved.

If you find yourself wondering
why the One would choose to appear as the Many,
try playing a game of chess by yourself.

If all is truly one,
then what is it that underlies both fear and love?

What we call love and fear are two states of awareness:
one which says, "I see this as myself,"
and the other which says, "I see this as other than myself."

But whether you see a thing as yourself or not,
the unifying element is the fact of your seeing.

Reality also possesses a certain vision or awareness of itself,
and the purest form of that awareness manifests
as a willingness to allow All That Is to be As It Is.

And that willingness we call Love.

So to step into Love means to step into the willingness
to allow something to be as it is. And in doing so, you
merge your own vision and awareness with that of Reality.

By contrast, when you fear or desire a thing, you are not
really seeing it. Its essence remains invisible to you, and
what you end up perceiving is the projection of your own
feeling onto it.

And this feeling is itself based on your response to a
memory, an impression formed through your own
conditioned awareness of a past event.

So when you relate to something through fear or desire,
know that you are not actually relating to it,
but to yourself.

If you were to awaken,
one fine aeon,
within the garden of Infinity,
would you not naturally desire to know
the sole delight denied to your awareness?

We have arrived here in this place of places
to taste the infinite fecundity
erupting at the edge of Self and Other,
as much as we have come to recollect
all that we are, and let go into oneness.

For oneness and relationship are but
the in-breath and the out-breath of the All.

So do not hate or fear your fear too much,
for were it not for this unwanted gift,
you would remain unbounded and untouched.

And know that fear, too, is a form of love . . .

For even as we flee, fight, curse, condemn,
and cast spells of Not-I upon the world,
we do so out of unremitting love
for that with which we do identify.

And though we steal, conceal, and re-reveal
this underlying secret to ourselves,
still secretly we long to be discovered,
unmasked for who and what we were and are,
and loved for all we have
and have not done.

About the Author

Eric Micha'el Leventhal is a literary consultant and holistic educator on the island of Maui, Hawai'i. A graduate of Stanford University and San Diego's International Professional School of Bodywork, he lived and journeyed extensively in Japan, Brazil, India and elsewhere before trading everything for love.

57400865R00076

Made in the USA
Middletown, DE
03 August 2019